SELF-CARE

A Simple Self-Care Guide to Rid Yourself of Anxiety, Stress and Achieve Happiness.

Table of Contents

Foreword. 2

Chapter 1. What Self-Care Is. What it isn't. 4

Chapter 2. The difference between self-improvement and self-care. 13

Chapter 3. Different Aspects of Self-Care. 16

Chapter 4. How to prioritize self-care. 41

Chapter 5. Self-care during stressful times. 45

Chapter 6. Steps for creating a self-care plan. 50

Afterword. 55

Do you secretly feel as if your life is dangling on the edge of a cliff? Are you constantly weighed down by the demands and responsibilities of your personal life, marriage and work?

Deep inside you know your emotional and psychological state are in a state of disarray due to neglect.

Your health too screams out for attention, and with each passing day, you gravitate further and further away from fitness. Because your health is weak, it explains why the gauge on your energy levels reads zero most of the time.

And yet, on the outside, you seem to be holding everything together pretty well.

But, you can't quite scratch that incessant itch that beckons there's more to life than just running the hamster wheel of daily demands.

Here's the good news-you're absolutely right. And here's the best news-you've come to the right place!

I thank and congratulate you for putting yourself first by downloading this e-book.

This self-care guide contains tips and ideas to help you gain and retain control of your life.

It also shows proven strategies and steps to assist you enhance and improve every aspect of your life.

In these pages, you'll discover examples of routines that you can begin to incorporate into your life to free yourself from the web of stress and anxiety.

You'll learn how to cut the cord of bad habits, how to establish your boundaries and how to fuel your inner resources.

And what's great is that you'll find an outline of the steps you need to create a personalized self-care plan.

My hope in creating this guide is to help you transform your life into a fulfilling, wholesome and happy existence.

I hope you enjoy it and thanks again for downloading!

Chapter 1.

What Self-Care Is. What it isn't.

If your life is like any of us mortals, it's full of errands, responsibilities, and chores that are all screaming for your attention. With such hectic lives, we end up feeling overwhelmed, depleted and disoriented.

That's because we spread ourselves too thin. But what does that even mean?

You know you've spread yourself too thin when your calendar is full and your to-do list resembles an endless circus.

When too many people are counting on you than you could possibly accommodate. Or when work life has taken over to an extent of encroaching on your personal space.

And while committing yourself to all of it may feel like a noble act, the truth is that you only sacrifice yourself. Without the right routines to provide an anchor, you end up digging a hole for yourself.

Because the truth is, you need to have a full cup before you can pour yourself into others. Just like in airplanes, you must attend to yourself before assisting others.

You see, when your life is overwhelmed, it leaves little or no room to nourish your mind, soul, and body. As a result, you begin to experience a decline in your overall well-being.

Because like everything else, failing to nurture your health, leads to rapid disintegration.

For starters, your immunity begins to plummet. It doesn't take long to become susceptible to flu and the common cold. Without exercise, other sicknesses slowly creep in. In no time, you find yourself in the perilous zone for high blood pressure, diabetes and heart disease.

But that's not all.

Part of the ripple effect of this is that it takes a toll on your energy levels.

As you begin to plummet, your productivity subsequently fizzles out. Which in turn, impacts your productivity well as well as your financial stability.

When you're depleted, you are basically running on low as far as your natural resources are concerned. Your inner strength, drive, and will are almost non-existent.

You've got no more wind in your sails.

From then onwards, you lose your inner balance.

And that's not a pretty place to be in. Because losing your inner balance means you've nothing to cling to. No anchor. No support. No shield.

This precarious position, if not nipped at the bud, leads to an even worse situation; Stress, and anxiety- an awfully dangerous place to be in.

This is because stress is the monster eating us up more than anything else in the modern-day. The inability to manage the demands and responsibilities of your life increases the production of the stress hormone cortisol.

Cortisol then increases your stress levels which then makes you prone to anxiety.

Sure, to a certain degree, you can contain the stress that comes from your responsibilities. However, the truth is some stress triggers are beyond your control.

But here's the thing; you can totally control how you react towards them. The key is finding that sweet spot of balance between stress and anxiety and your happiness.

This self-care guide explains how you can begin to give yourself the care you need to navigate through life in these stressful times.

Because whilst the responsibilities in your life must be attended to, it is paramount that you replenish at the same time. This way, you not only safeguard your overall well-being but you're also able to function at your optimal potential.

But, how exactly can you do that?

Well... I'm glad you asked.

Enter self-care.

For most of us, the term self-care connotes scented candles, essential oils, and bubble baths - all good stuff. But really, the true meaning of self-care extends far beyond the bubble baths, massages, and spas treatments.

Self-care can be defined as the habits and attitudes consciously geared towards taking care of your emotional, mental and physical health.

Simply put, self-care is giving yourself love. It's putting yourself first. It's filling your cup. It's refuelling your inner reserves. It's all these, done in a deeper, consistent and more fulfilling way.

Good self-care is also fundamental for positive mood, reduced stress and decreased anxiety.

Though it's a simple concept, in theory, it's a practice we very regularly overlook.

In fact, the essence of self-care is so essential that it should ultimately be an integral component of your life.

Because really, what good is a luxurious massage with the most expensive essential oils when your health is going down the drain?

Even worse, what pleasure can be derived from a pampered spa treatment when your mental health is in disarray?

Contrary to what many of us think, self-care isn't a selfish act. We confuse self-care with being egocentric — that somehow looking after ourselves is self-indulgence as opposed to a self-respectful act.

Because when you engage in self-care practices, you're not just thinking about your needs. Instead, you're creating the right atmosphere to better cope with yourself and subsequently extend care to others.

It goes without saying that if you are incapable of nurturing yourself, you won't be in the right state of mind to cater to your cherished ones either.

However, with more energy and extra reserve, you can work better and give back to your community.

Because the biggest benefit of self-care is to promote your well-being, a huge part of that means being able to process your emotional experience.

The way to do that is to ensure that you create the time to sift through your emotions.

Learn how to connect with what's going on inside you. Learn how to gain emotional clarity such that you can pinpoint the state of your emotions at any given time.

Unfortunately, most people think of self-care as a means of distracting or numbing their emotions.

As such, they engage in activities such as binge-watching TV or losing themselves in a hobby. And while this can work for a while, it doesn't address your real need; that of connecting with your emotions.

For this reason, it's best to evaluate the outcome of your self-care routine. Does it usher in a higher perspective? Does it give you emotional release? Is there any positive progress at an inner level?

These questions are crucial in determining if you're engaging in the right self-care habits.

When people hear the concept of self-care, they imagine it to be a practice or lifestyle too demanding to accommodate. They feel that they don't have the time to devote to self-care routines.

And while this is true to some extent- because you would need to organize your schedule in order to slot in self-care – it's really not what self-care entails.

You see, self-care is a lifestyle you adopt for the rest of your life. It gels with your existence. It stays with you. Daily.

It's the anchor you build in order to find stability in your life. Self-care becomes the axis you position yourself to so that you can gain and retain control of your life.

The question then is; self-care is so vital, why are we all not doing it?

Well, for starters, our lives are too busy. Way too busy. Our personal demands, career duties, marital and parenting responsibilities are constantly beckoning for our attention at every turn.

Our jobs are also stressful and very demanding. In addition, technology has taken over a huge chunk of our lives leaving us little or no private time.

Also, given that the notion of self-care is laced with the underlying misconception that it's a selfish act, we rarely put ourselves first because that very notion makes us uncomfortable.

But on the subtle side of self-care, lies the biggest reason why we deny ourselves this essential care.

You see, self-care requires us to have a certain degree of self-awareness, and many of us are not willing to take that route.

For you to become self-aware, you need to be in touch with your feelings - both negative and positive.

However, as humans, we are wired to steer clear of anything that awakens bad feelings within us.

In fact, research shows that fear is just a self-defence mechanism, geared to make us change course when we come too close to something that triggers an element of discomfort.

Because of that, we are reluctant to get in touch with our raw feelings especially the negative ones.

Unfortunately avoiding them is counter-productive. Since retreating doesn't address the problems or reveal the changes we need to make to put ourselves first.

As such, we end up sacrificing self-care.

In as much as self-care can - and will - alter the trajectory of your life, the reality is, you'll need to put in a bit of work.

You may have to go to some discomfiting places deep within you.

Perhaps iron a few rough edges by making a few adjustments in your life. All this calls for a certain level of discipline and focus to push through the necessary changes.

But once you jump past those hurdles, the sun in your life will begin to shine. You'll begin to gain clarity as the perspective about your life starts to shift.

This is the first step towards getting rid of the stress and anxiety that weigh you down. This same step creates an avenue for happiness and peace.

Chapter 2.

The difference between self-improvement and self-care.

Self-improvement is often mistaken for self-care, even though they're subtly different.

The foundation of self-improvement stands on a perfectionist mindset. Meaning, you hold off appreciating and embracing yourself until you arrive at your desired goal.

For instance, not feeling worthy of yourself until you look a certain way, achieve a certain goal, or lose a specific number of kilos.

Unfortunately, this misplaced notion has been breathed down on us for so long. Look around.

You see it all the time from the components of the self-development industry, such as weight-reduction plan and weight loss programs.

The common underlying message is that if we work harder and locate our discipline, we'll be capable of fixing what feels defective, and only then will we be worthy of honourable lives.

This by itself is an unhealthy perspective, one that does more harm than good.

Because, if for some reason you fail short of achieving your set goal, you inevitably move into a disgrace spiral. You then start to tell yourself that you are not good or sufficient enough.

But self-care is an entirely different ballgame.

Because the principle of self-care is based on self-acceptance. And that's self-acceptance right now. Not tomorrow when every star in your life aligns, but at this moment.

You see, it's magical when you embrace yourself without the pressure of futuristic goals that self-improvement gives you.

When you do that, you are telling yourself that you're still worthy of self-care even as you work your way towards the goals you've set for yourself.

So, how do you go about that?

The best place to start is by doing some introspection.

This requires you to take a long hard look at the scope of your life and see if all the parts of the puzzle fit together harmoniously.

Check if you're working toward a holistic life. Figure out which parts of your life are functioning well.

Ask yourself if you're honestly fulfilled with how your life is playing out or if you need to iron out a few rough edges.

Once you've figured that out, you'll need to carve out the time to engage in activities that will gradually liberate yourself from the entangling web of stress and anxiety imposed by the demands of life.

The reality is, every one of these aspects is important and succeeding in only one area is not sufficient. You've got to find a balance. And this means incorporating all the aspects.

Next is a breakdown of all the aspects of your life and the best ways of incorporating self-care.

Chapter 3.

It's worth noting that the process of self-care encompasses three key aspects of your life; emotional, physical and mental.

And these three aspects are can be broken down into the following areas.

Physical self-care.

Physical self-care means you're taking good care of your body.

This is the most essential form of self-care because, without good health, you have nothing. Because your body is the vessel that carries you in the journey of life. And we all know a broken vessel just won't do the job right.

Physical self-care tips:

Eat right.

This includes nourishing your body by eating healthy and nutritious food. Opt for whole foods that fuel your body and give you energy for the day.

Your body has no choice but to serve you if you nourish it well.

Water is also a vital part of self-care.

Studies have shown that dehydration leads to the elevation of levels of the stress hormone cortisol.

This means that when you are dehydrated, you are more prone to stress.

Drinking water also sends many ripple effects such as clear skin and increased energy. Also, water keeps your weight in check.

Move more.

Exercise doesn't have to be painful and torturous to be effective. A simple act such as taking thirty minutes' walks can do wonders for your body. This is a game-changer because you stand to benefit in huge ways.

For starters, it's a simple, enjoyable and effective way to keep you from lifestyle illnesses such as heart disease, diabetes, and stroke.

A walk also gives you the chance to escape into your own world, where it's just you and your thoughts.

It's in these moments of solitude that clarity trickles in the most. This way you can get a clear perspective of the state of your life and evaluate the changes that need to be made.

This also improves your mood significantly and sets you up for a good day.

Sleep enough.

Because your body needs to rejuvenate, it's paramount to have adequate sleep. Good quality sleep not only empowers you for a productive day, but it also nourishes your mind.

There's a connection between your mind and your body and this is why it's important to give your mind enough rest.

Clean up!

You may hit the gym seven times a week, and get those toned abs- which is everybody's dream- but to complete the picture, you must clean up. This is where hygiene and grooming come in. It's the cherry on top.

Ensure you maintain a clean body and keep your hair neat. While you are at it, keep those nails short – this is a must for men.

As for the ladies, short nails are much easier to maintain, but if your preference is long nails, remember to keep them clean and smooth.

While it may not seem as much, the impact is huge. Why? Because good hygiene and grooming make you socially acceptable.

Think about it.

When you're clean and well-groomed, your self-esteem is automatically elevated because you feel good about yourself. It adds a spring to your step.

In the same breath, you attract people towards you, and this elicits a ripple effect; it heightens your self-worth. High self-worth transforms you into a happier, more confident and less stressed version of yourself.

I hope you can begin to see just how much your quality of life is greatly impacted by practicing physical self-care.

This transformation not only alters your body but it also radically improves your relationships.

Me-time.

It goes without saying that relationships are your greatest assets in life.

However, many of us are guilty of overlooking the importance of one of the greatest, most important relationships you can ever have. And that's a relationship with yourself.

The best way to create a relationship with yourself is to have some me-time. This means you carve out some time for self-care on your calendar.

This is your alone-time. No distractions. No responsibilities. No kids. No partner. Just you and yourself.

This is a sacred time where you connect with your inner self. Here, you examine the course of your life through the lens of your authentic perspective.

Your me-time creates an avenue to organize your thoughts. It helps you figure out what's working in your life and what's not. It helps you to create cracks through which clarity can seep through.

And as clarity trickles in, you'll find yourself dislodging the issues that have been unsettling your mind.

In so many ways, me-time is bringing power back to yourself.

So how do you go about it?

Simple. Start by pampering yourself. Plan a date night with yourself and relax in the ambiance of soothing music. You can also or engage in a hobby.

We all have that one thing we loved doing when we were kids. Do that. Is it painting, knitting, drawing, dancing? Do whatever makes you come alive. You'll be surprised how much this can revitalize you.

Remember to treat this time as sacrosanct and non-negotiable.

Spiritual self-care.

Spiritual self-care comprises of intentional actions we take to strengthen our connection with our higher-self. Our higher self is the part that defines who we really are.

At the core of this part, is your inner fulfilment, tranquillity, and peace. Spiritual self-care will lead you on the path towards alignment with your core values.

Spiritual self-care tips:

Prayer.

For centuries, men and women have used the practice of prayer to bring calmness and healing for the soul by seeking divine guidance.

When you take the time to express your deepest feelings to God through faith, you experience calmness peace from within. By letting go of your worries, you're able to reduce stress and anxiety from your life.

Meditation.

Meditation involves calming your thoughts and quietening your inner chatter.

This is of great benefit as it helps you to evaluate your life in a more comprehensive way by raising your self-realization. Through meditation, you can reduce stress and anxiety by increasing your level of enlightenment.

Gratitude.

Your best approach to this is to create a gratitude journal. Here, you note down all the things, events and occurrences you are grateful for.

This way, you become more cognizant of the many wonderful things you would normally not take notice of.

This, in turn, raises your vibration and creates a ripple effect. The more grateful you are, the more you attract more things to be grateful for.

Emotional self-care.

Your emotions are a mirror of what's happening to you. Both external and internal factors play a key role in the state of your emotions.

While you may not always control the factors that trigger your emotions, you can totally control how your emotions influence you.

In order to maintain a happy and positive mindset, it is vital to master the art of managing your emotions.

When you adopt a healthy mindset about your emotions and the best way of managing them, it places you in the axis of control.

And isn't that what you want?

As such, rather than collapsing every time a strong feeling descends on you like an avalanche, you're able to adjust your stance and evaluate the situation objectively.

This is how you reclaim your crown of control. And it goes a long way to ensure you don't drown in self-inflicted guilt and helplessness.

Emotional self-care tips:

Be self-aware.

Self-awareness is becoming more knowledgeable of your emotions and character.

The beauty of self-awareness is that it holds a mirror to your face and helps you to automatically become sensitized to your emotions.

This way, you can pinpoint the state of your emotions at any given time. Most importantly, you're able to identify the triggers behind each of them.

You understand the events, people, and things that are related to them.

When you become self-aware, it unearths a better understanding of your character. You have a better understanding of why you act in the manner that you do.

But perhaps the most important aspect of self-awareness is that it assists you to decide which way to behave when a scenario arises.

This is because each time a specific emotion is expressed, it offers you another opportunity to examine yourself and respond in a manner that feels proper.

This way, your emotions are not like a reed swayed by any emotional wind.

What this does, is that it develops your character, making you grounded and mature.

Create boundaries.

Let's face it, another reason why our lives are super stressful is attributed to the mountains of demands that surround us.

But here's the sad reality; most of the demands in our lives are not self-imposed, but are rather the creation of others.

These demands are often from our partners, children, parents, employers, and friends. We're often running the hamster wheel as we try to fulfil each one of these demands.

Most of us gravitate towards people-pleasing to maintain peace and cohesiveness. And whilst we may not realize it, each time we drain ourselves trying to fulfil other peoples' needs, is also how we shoot ourselves in the foot; we violate our emotional integrity.

Does that sound like you?

If so, don't despair. There's a way to navigate this exhausting maze.

Enter boundaries.

You see, creating healthy boundaries is the only way to protect your emotional integrity. People-pleasing is spreading yourself too thin. And it leaves you depleted and anxious, eventually, you're unable to cope with the demands.

By creating boundaries, you erect a wall that shields you from living a stressful and anxious life. Boundaries are essentially the armour you use to protect yourself from emotional invasion.

But that's not all.

Boundaries are extremely vital because they give people an indication of how to treat you. When you enforce boundaries, you are basically drawing a line in the sand, making it clear what the parameters of your life are.

You are differentiating what's acceptable to you from what's not. The fact is, you are ultimately responsible for how people treat you.

Listen to your gut.

Your gut is your inner voice. It's that part of you that bears witness when no one is watching. As part of your emotional self-care, you need to tune in to the antennae of your gut. Because it will often tell you things that nobody else will.

Your gut feeling looks like this:

A sinking feeling when you see a certain person. Or an unsettling emotion when you enter a certain room.

Or perhaps an anxious feeling that rises to your heart when you think of attending a specific social gathering.

These are all feelings that arise within you every so often- perhaps even daily.

You mustn't ignore them. Because it's your body communicating and sending signals to alert you of things you need to steer clear of.

As you hearken to your gut, you'll distance yourself from people, events, and situations that don't serve you.

This will go a long way to keep away from stress, anxiety while also safeguarding your happiness.

Vocational or work self-care.

If you are employed, chances are, you are devoting a huge chunk of your life to your work.

It's even worse if you're building your own empire because you're probably clocking in hundreds of hours towards your hustle. Over and above the average employee.

There's absolutely nothing wrong with that.

The problem arises when you can't strike a balance between your ever-demanding work life and taking care of yourself.

By compromising your self-care, you upset the cart that could potentially wreak havoc on your well-being.

This is why the practice of self-care should be a daily routine. Because the misconception that you can beat yourself up all week and pamper yourself over the weekend is just that, a misconception.

It holds no water and it doesn't work.

So, what works?

What works is incorporating spaces of rest between your work responsibilities. In fact, it's necessary because to be productive, your brain and body need small breaks.

This is how you strike a balance.

The truth is, regardless of whether you work in an office setting, or within the confines of your home, it's possible to achieve a self-care routine.

These tips will show you how to do just that.

Work self-care tips:

Be proactive.

When it comes to self-care, becoming proactive means taking the first steps to promote a more relaxed work-life. This means eliminating situations that would otherwise make you stressed and anxious.

A perfect example would be to attend to your tasks first. Eat your frog!

If you're an employee, it helps to figure out what is needed of you and then getting into the business of doing it as promptly as you can.

Because when you own your responsibilities, it keeps your boss from breathing down your neck.

How good is that?

The added bonus? It puts you in good books with your employer and also adds a zing to your professional life.

You stand to gain the same benefit of proactiveness even if you work from home. Because part of being proactive demands that you develop a feasible plan; one that will help you balance the responsibilities of your home with those of your work.

This is best done by planning your tasks ahead of time, and allocating a time slot for each. It's always best to start with your priorities. This way, you're organized and prepared in your problem-spotting and solving.

Protect your lunch-hour.

Your lunch hour is extremely precious, sacred even – I am willing to bet you know that already.

But, there's so much more you could do with your lunch hour.

It doesn't have to be just about food. Your lunch hour is the time to disconnect from the outside and connect with yourself.

It can be the time you relax in the fresh air and allow your mind a slice of peace and calm away from the hustle and bustle of work.

This can be your time to exhale and engage in acts that uplifts you. For example, reading a book, listening to a podcast, going for a run. Or whatever works for you. This will not only fuel you but will accelerate your productivity later in the day.

Harness work relationships.

As social creatures, our need for relationships is ingrained in us.

But there's a slight twist- one that we often miss - you don't just need relationships. You need, healthy interpersonal relationships. You need human connections that enhance you and empower you. These are key to your mental health and longevity.

Because you spend a considerable chunk of your life in your workplace, with the same people, it's worth investing a bit of effort to harness a basic relationship at the very least. Sure, sometimes this can feel like walking a tight rope since some of your peers might not be compatible with your personality.

However, harnessing a basic relationship might only require you to devote just five minutes in the morning to say hello to your co-workers. It may even be as easy as dragging a colleague out for a cup of tea.

Once in a while, take an hour or two every few weeks to drop by happy hour.

It'll make your days that much rewarding and your job more fulfilling.

Social self-care.

Although socialization is very important to your mental well-being, it's often challenging to make time for friends. Due to busy schedules, it's easy to neglect your relationships.

Given that connections are vital for your well-being, cultivating and preserving close relationships calls for you to invest time and energy into them.

The reason being - just like everything else — relationships, when not nurtured and attended to, wither and die.

There's no set number of hours needed to spend time nurturing your relationships. The most important thing is to determine the value a relationship is adding to your life. Once that's done, you'll be able to work around your schedules.

Social self-care tips:

Reach out.

So. We've already established the need of social life for your mental and emotional well-being.

The question now becomes; how do you build a tribe of your own?

Sometimes you need to be proactive and reach out to others. For example, you can offer to accompany your neighbour or colleague to the gym or yoga class. You can also call an acquaintance and say hello now and then.

This is also your opportunity to intentionally reconnect with someone you've not connected with for a long while. Or one that you have unsettled warfare with.

You'll be surprised how responsive people are.

Do fun stuff.

In order to create and expand your social circle/tribe, it helps to maintain good engagement consistently. This is the only way you can build relationships that will last. When you plan and incorporate fun stuff in your meetings, you create a happy atmosphere.

Picnics are a good example. You can also choose to visit a nature trail closest to you. While you are at it, you and your friend might want to take your pets out and introduce them to each other.

Movie nights are great for fostering good relationships. Perhaps even take some swimming sessions together. The list is endless, really.

Make an impact.

One of the most satisfying feelings has to be the ability to bring a smile to someone's face. This is what truly touches humanity. And the best thing of all? It works both ways.

When you leave a positive impact on someone's life, the same happiness finds a way of radiating back to you.

As the saying goes, people never forget how you make them feel. That means that for one person you impact, you've made yourself a friend.

You could visit an aged care facility and spend the day with them. You could also volunteer at rehabilitation homes.

You could offer your skills and expertise to drug rehabilitation centres and provide value in some sort of way. Perhaps you could consider registering in a guide institution for people going through what you've gone through.

By making an impact in society, you'll be amazed at your potential to be valuable to other peoples' lives. This is exactly how you can grow your tribe and harness your social life.

Financial self-care.

The internet is brimming with information about finances. From how to budget, save, spend and everything in between.

However, in the midst of all these, is a glaring need to address how your emotions attach to cash, as well as your internal beliefs surrounding finances.

It is paramount to understand and define your emotions about finances because the reality is, money is essential to our lives.

Because most of us grew up with a lack of money, over-time, we created these self-limiting beliefs about our relationship with money.

However, holding onto these beliefs restricts you and leaves you stressed out and anxious. This, in turn, affects your quality of life keeping you from having a full life.

As such, it's vital to re-write the narratives you've created over the years.

Financial self-care tips:

Sure, you make time for your other emotions but do you really analyse your emotions as relates to finances? What's your perspective on money? Do you believe you can have a healthy relationship with money? Or are you convinced that money is evil?

Really evaluate your beliefs to identify any deep-rooted ideologies that pertain to money. Ask yourself if they are based on the truth at all.

As you do the evaluation, you'll be able to filter any negative connotations which might be otherwise ingrained in you.

Be brutally honest and transparent with yourself about your income.

Look, it's impossible to practice financial self-care if you don't have a clear perspective of how much you're working with.

Sure, you probably know what your pay check says but that's not enough. You need to get clear on all your earnings.

For example, take into account the bonuses you receive and the proceeds from your side gig. When you have an accurate feel of your overall income, it will help you to monitor and expand your financial base.

Be accountable.

And no, this doesn't mean becoming excessively frugal with your spending.

Instead, it just means tracking your finances. This way, you're able to determine whether you're putting your money in the right place.

Avoid falling into the trap of splurging on the latest trends instead, ensure you're spending money things and causes that enhance your well-being.

For instance a self-help book, gym membership, and cooking classes.

Physiological self-care.

Never in the past has there been such a dire need to prioritize psychological self-care as in the times you're living in now. Primarily because you're bombarded with stresses from all angles. To say it can leave you drained and exhausted is an understatement.

These can have an adverse effect on your relationships, physical health, work, finances and your quality of life. But perhaps the worst-case scenario is the effect they can have on your mental health.

This is one more reason why you must begin to look at self-care differently. You have to change your perception of self-care as a one-time thing and assimilate it into your lifestyle.

Because the sad reality is, these stresses and anxieties are not going away any time soon.

In fact, chances are, with the world-changing as fast as it is, we are likely to experience an upsurge of the same.

Fortunately, there's a way around it. And it starts with shielding yourself from it all. True, you might not be able to entirely avoid these stresses, but you can build habits that will help you steer clear of the triggers.

Psychological self-care tips:

Minimize social media.

The paradox of social media is it's both an asset and a liability. Social media can take your life notches high and can also bury you in the dark hole of comparison.

The sad reality is that the majority tend to gravitate towards the latter. The tentacles of the wrong side of social media have pierced through the lives of many, throwing their psychological stability into disarray.

For this reason, minimizing the time you spend scrolling through your social media feed is crucial.

Sure, at first you might experience FOMO (fear of missing out), but in reality, that's a very small price to pay. You stand to gain so much more in return.

For example, you're able to focus on your life.

I mean properly, without any external distractions. This way, you are no longer living your life from the lens of other peoples' experiences, but you're genuinely focused on you.

You're also able to scale up your productivity.

Why? Because minimizing social media can free up so much of your time. This allows you to be creative and innovative.

When your brain is engaged in a creative endeavour, you're able to derive a lot of satisfaction. It does your mental well-being a great deal of good.

Get in touch with yourself.

In order to replenish your cup, you need to hit pause and reset. You need to slam the door on everything that doesn't nourish your essence.

Find time to be alone and connect with yourself. Go for a walk alone and soak up in the beauty of nature. You'll experience a trickle of clarity streaming into your conscience.

Go to a café, order your cup of tea and read a book. Give yourself a date night every week to connect with yourself.

Over time, you'll start to reap the benefits of a renewed perspective and outlook in yourself and your life in general.

Lose yourself.

Sometimes the best way to find yourself is to lose yourself.

Sounds confusing right? Allow me to explain.

You see, when you find something you enjoy doing and lose yourself to it, you subconsciously cut the cord that ties you to your daily stresses and anxieties.

It's by decreasing your level of stress that you're able to raise mental fitness and happiness.

When you identify the thing that makes you come alive, lose yourself to it. Be it a dance, a show or painting sessions. Do it least once a week and when you do it, stay engaged and intentional about it.

Are you finding this book helpful and enjoyable?

Kindly leave a review here.

https://www.amazon.com/review/create-review/

Chapter 4.

So, by now you know how critical self-care is to your overall well-being-which is great. But like all things, consistency is key. This is what moves the needle. This is what will set the tone for you to live your life effectively.

For you to be consistent in your self-care practices, you'll need to make it a priority.

But how do you do that? How do you make sure you're slotting in self-care somewhere in your otherwise very tight schedule?

Below are tips to assist you in prioritizing self-care.

Slot it in your calendar.

As humans, we get things done better and faster when they are in some sort of structure. The same is true for self-care. Slot down the activities in your calendar. Allocate some time for each one. By doing so, you're bound to follow through more regularly.

Carve out 10 minutes just for you.

It's one thing to schedule some self-care time, it's another thing altogether too actually follow through.

Reality is, there will always be distractions, people, and demands crying out for your attention. It's easy to postpone or forego your intentions entirely.

Sure, at first it might not be that big of a deal, but if this happens often, what happens is that you're more likely to end up abandoning self-care completely.

For this reason, it's crucial to carve out 10-15 minutes to yourself on a daily basis. Not an hour or more. Just 10-15 minutes to connect with yourself and evaluate what you need.

You can surely afford just 10-15 minutes every day. As a matter of fact, the people in your life will understand if you are unavailable for 15 minutes.

Disconnect.

Are you finally doing something that puts wind in your sails? Good. Now disconnect from all distractions. Steer clear of your computer. Unplug your landline if you need to.

If self-care to you means reading or going for yoga with your new friend, ensure you switch off your phone. Leave it in the car if you can. Quit checking your work emails and social media feeds.

This way, you'll be engaged and even enjoy yourself a little bit more.

At the end of the day, there's no point in blocking everyone out only to end up swallowed up in the bottomless pit of social media and the web.

Sleep.

If you're going to achieve any breakthrough in your self-care habits, it's extremely important to get proper, good quality sleep. Your body needs a good chunk of sleep to rejuvenate. This is how you heal, both physically and mentally.

Because a sleep-deprived body is as cranky as a grumpy old man, chances are you'll only upset those around you-including those you're trying to foster good relationships with.

A night of good sleep will ensure your state of mind is both alert and calm. This way, you're ready to participate fully in your self-care practice. You're strong enough for that dance, yoga, gym session or the cooking class.

Reward yourself.

So you've been consistent with your newly formed self-care habits? Great job.

Now it's time to reward yourself. Get out and treat yourself to that new pair of shoes. Buy those rose flowers, then put them in a vase on your dressing mirror. Treat yourself to a massage at that luxurious spa.

Chapter 5.

At the onset of a self-care lifestyle, most of us approach it with heightened enthusiasm. We do everything right. We maintain consistency.

But as you know, life always seems to have an agenda of its own and it damn well pushes that agenda on our path. This is what upsets the apple cart.

It can leave you feeling disoriented and within no time, throw in the towel. This can have adverse effects on your physical and mental health. With time, you slowly re-coil to the mould of your former life.

As such, it's extremely vital to double up on self-care during stressful times. Without a doubt, it can be a tall order to balance self-care when you're already drowning in stress. But this is when you need to pull up your sleeves.

Here's how to go about it.

Strategize.

At times, your source of stress may be triggered by tight deadlines such as pending projects or exams. Whatever these may be, strategic planning is your best friend. You see when you plan, you're calmer and less anxious.

Part of strategizing should include setting micro-goals and allocating a time to execute them. Make them as small and manageable.

Taking in too much will make you feel overwhelmed and it's more likely that you won't accomplish any.

Tick them off once accomplished. The more progress you make, the more relaxed you feel. The bonus of strategizing is that it boosts your productivity.

Let yourself feel it.

Our natural tendency, when faced with stress, is to flee from it. We avoid it, tiptoe around it and even ignore the cause of it.

But when you really think about it, that's counter-productive. Because eventually, it catches upon us. We can only run so far.

Sometimes, acknowledging and facing the triggers head-on is the best thing you can do for yourself.

Why?

Because the process of figuring out what's wrong and the appropriate ways to manage it can only be achieved through self-reflection.

While going through it may not feel like self-care, it's often the beginning of self-care. Because once you're done figuring out what's wrong, you can then go about the business of fixing it.

Communicate.

Each one of us has a mechanism of coping with stress depending on our personalities. But irrespective of this, one thing is clear, we should all let it out.

Venting is great as it relieves the pressure off your mind. It can be very therapeutic to your emotional and mental health.

It's important to be selective with the person whom you vent out to. Ideally, you want to share the stresses of your life with someone trustworthy. Someone who will support you and preferably offer some valuable advice.

Talk to yourself.

The loudest voice is the one inside your head. It's often the one that wins.

This is why it's important to be intentional about what you tell yourself. In stressful times, you need to speak to yourself more frequently.

Compliment yourself, encourage yourself and speak good things about yourself throughout the day.

Tell yourself things like 'I am worthy, I am strong, I am victorious'.

Do this irrespective of your reality. Eventually, your mind will accept it as a reality. When you send out positive energy, it starts to impact your circumstances, events and people around you in a positive way.

Things begin to look up and the stress fizzles out slowly. This is when everything changes and you start to feel better.

Get comfortable saying NO.

In so many ways, saying NO is means saying YES.

At times, there's only so much you can take, especially when grappling with stressful issues.

Because stress can leave you depleted, you might need to build your walls up high to protect yourself.

During such times, your assertiveness needs to come to play more than ever. You need to be ok with saying no to tasks, meetings, responsibilities and even people who stretch you beyond your capacity.

Remember it's perfectly ok to drop the ball.

Don't feel like getting out for that night out with your friends? Then don't. Turn in early if you need to.

Chapter 6.

The best way to ensure your zeal doesn't wither like leaves in winter is to develop a plan. A self-care plan gives you structure and control. This means that your life is not chaotic.

So how can you create a self-care plan that is both effective and manageable?

The steps outlined below will guide you.

Step 1. Evaluate your current self- care routines.

It's possible to have existing self-care routines and not even be aware. If you were to take a closer look, you'd probably identify some routines in your life patterns. A good place to start would be to evaluate your coping mechanisms.

For example, what habits, routines or things do you engage in to make your existence more wholesome?

Once you identify them, aim to evaluate the effectiveness of each one.

Try to determine if a particular self-care practice opens a channel towards connecting with your emotions-because this is the most authentic way to pinpoint your stressors.

Or whether it numbs you-which is counterproductive and ineffective.

By taking a closer look at your self-care routines, things will swim into focus and you'll be able to have a clear perspective of what's working and what's not.

The outcome of this evaluation will take you to the next step.

Step 2. Make the necessary adjustments.

So. You've got a pretty good perspective of the effectiveness of your self-care practices – or a lack of it.

Now it's time to make the necessary adjustments. You'll need to double up on the good side of your self-care practices and eliminate the futile ones.

This is also the time to weed out the barriers standing between you and your goals. At this point, you need to start changing the pattern and disconnecting from what no longer serves you.

As part of making the necessary adjustments, you'll also need to determine if these self-care practices balance out properly in the scope of your life.

Why?

Because a good balance is key for your wholesome well-being. Devoting all your time and attention to one aspect of your life and neglecting the rest will not work.

Step 3. Create an actual plan.

Once you've established the areas that need work, you'll need to take it a step further and create your personalized plan. One that fits well into the scope of your life.

Here, outline the initiatives against each aspect of your life.

For example:

Financial: Maintaining a sticking to a budget, keeping tabs on all my income sources, etc.

Social: Making time to go for walks with a friend, checking up on my friends regularly, etc.

Emotional: Connecting with myself daily through meditation and dealing with any stressors at the onset to avoid them escalating much later.

Writing it down gives you structure and helps you to maintain focus.

Step 4. Commit.

Once you've ironed out the rough edges, and structured it all in one document, it's now time to do the most important thing:

Make a commitment.

This is everything. It's what gets the job done. It's what brings about the change that's needed to uplift the standard of your life. When you commit to yourself, you're more likely to follow through.

The best approach to this is to write a commitment note and sign it. Then place it somewhere you can see every day. This continuous reminder will keep you tethered to your plan.

Also, it helps to share your self-care plan with a friend. Let them know what your intentions are in developing the plan.

They will hold you accountable and might even offer valuable tips to incorporate into your self-care plan.

Step 5. Evaluate.

Because things are bound to change, and life is unpredictable, make a point of evaluating your plan once in a while.

Check in to see if your plan is effective. Is it working for you or do you need to shift things a bit? Then, make any necessary changes.

Your self-care plan should help you to grow and upgrade your life. As such, you must not settle once you've achieved some goals. Without new challenges, growth doesn't happen.

Hence, you should aim to incorporate new self-care practices each year. Try something that pushes you out of your comfort zone. Learn a new skill, explore new ways to impact your community. Whatever. Push yourself and see how much your life will change.

Also, every year, celebrate your strides and reward yourself.

You can never be too motivated.

Afterword.

Thanks again for downloading this e-book.

I hope it has helped to shed some much-needed light because let's face it, never in the history of mankind has self-care become as critical as it is now.

Fortunately, you're now well equipped to begin incorporating self-care into your life. Your next step is to apply the strategies in the book.

But don't be too hard on yourself, start by setting small goals. That's what will get you there. Allow yourself as much time as you need to make the necessary changes.

As you make these changes, you'll also start to develop and nurture an intimate relationship with the most important person - yourself.

Lastly, if you enjoyed this book, please take a minute and share your thoughts by posting a review here:

https://www.amazon.com/review/create-review/

It will be greatly appreciated.

Thank you and good luck!

Leah Njoki

https://ownyourspark.com/

www.ingramcontent.com/pod-product-compliance
Lightning Source LLC
Chambersburg PA
CBHW030409160726
47992CB00007B/3037